CONTENTS

OUR WORLD IN PICTURES

SPACECRAFT

AN INTRODUCTION FOR CHILDREN FROM 6 TO 10

Conception
Emilie Beaumont

Text
Agnès Vandewiele

Translation
Linda Clement

Illustrations
Sebastian Quigley

FLEURUS

THE FIRST ROCKETS

During the eighth century, the Chinese invented the first rockets: small weapons to frighten their enemies. Using similar weapons loaded with explosives, the Englishman, Congreve, fought Napoleon at the battle of Waterloo in 1815. A century later, the American, Goddard, began sending rockets higher and higher into the sky. Finally, in 1944, with the V-2 aircraft which were used to drop bombs, the world saw the first real, flying rockets. After World War II, they were perfected to conquer space.

Jules Verne

In 1865 Jules Verne wrote in his book, *A Trip from the Earth to the Moon*, about three men traveling in space. Launched in a shell with a cone-shaped tip, they "camped in lunar solitudes." That long ago, he saw our future!

Chinese Rockets

These "fire arrows" concocted by the Chinese in the eighth century were the first rockets. Essentially cardboard cylinders loaded with black powder, they carried a small explosive charge in their tips. When the powder was ignited, these mini-rockets were hurled at their enemies. They were also used by the Mongols, then by the Arabs. The French saw them during their seventh crusade in Egypt.

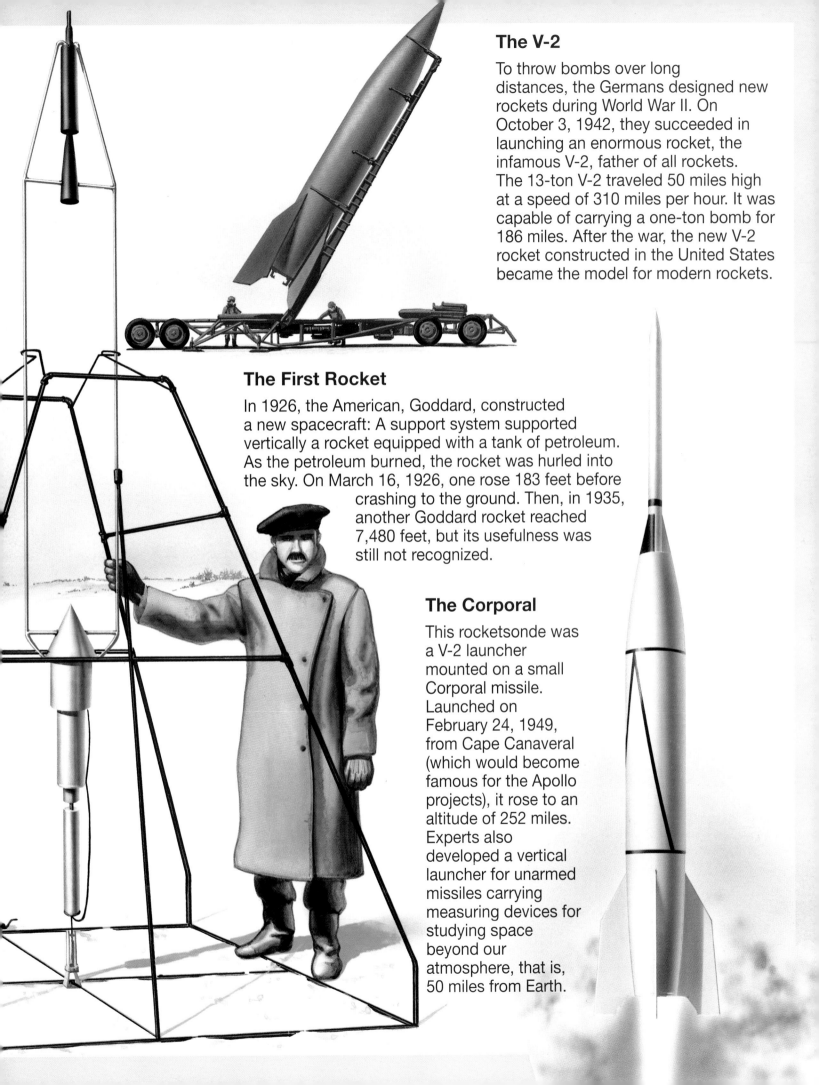

The V-2

To throw bombs over long distances, the Germans designed new rockets during World War II. On October 3, 1942, they succeeded in launching an enormous rocket, the infamous V-2, father of all rockets. The 13-ton V-2 traveled 50 miles high at a speed of 310 miles per hour. It was capable of carrying a one-ton bomb for 186 miles. After the war, the new V-2 rocket constructed in the United States became the model for modern rockets.

The First Rocket

In 1926, the American, Goddard, constructed a new spacecraft: A support system supported vertically a rocket equipped with a tank of petroleum. As the petroleum burned, the rocket was hurled into the sky. On March 16, 1926, one rose 183 feet before crashing to the ground. Then, in 1935, another Goddard rocket reached 7,480 feet, but its usefulness was still not recognized.

The Corporal

This rocketsonde was a V-2 launcher mounted on a small Corporal missile. Launched on February 24, 1949, from Cape Canaveral (which would become famous for the Apollo projects), it rose to an altitude of 252 miles. Experts also developed a vertical launcher for unarmed missiles carrying measuring devices for studying space beyond our atmosphere, that is, 50 miles from Earth.

THE FIRST MANNED FLIGHTS

The Americans and Russians began competing to send the first man into space. After vertically launching rockets, a new step awaited: tilting them horizontally to circle the earth at 17,400 miles per hour. They also needed to be able to carry and support human life in space. The Russians took the first step in November, 1957, by sending a dog, Laïka, around the earth in Sputnik 2. Laïka's voyage opened the door to man's fascinating adventure in space.

Yuri Gagarine
Only 25 years old, he was the first person to travel in space.

Yuri Gagarine was a Soviet army pilot. His feat made him famous around the world. In 1968, he died in an airplane accident.

The First Man in Space

This Russian space vessel, named Vostok, had two parts: the front, containing the cosmonaut's cabin which would be the only part to return to Earth, and the rear, the service module. On April 12, 1961, Yuri Gagarine settled inside Vostok 1, and, launched by the R-VII rocket, was shot into space at 7:07 A.M. He circled the earth at an altitude between 112 and 203 miles. Then, at 8:27 A.M., the cabin separated from the service module, returned to Earth, its parachute opened for landing. Vostok 1 and its occupant, Gagarine, landed at 8:55 A.M. in a field near Saratov in Russia. Man's first flight around the earth had lasted 108 minutes.

Vostok's Cabin

(left)

The Vostok cabin was a sphere measuring 7.5 feet across. Gagarine, wearing a spacesuit, sat in an ejectable seat. The air he breathed had the same composition as the earth's air.

John Glenn

John Glenn was 39 years old at the time of his first exploit. This trial pilot was chosen by NASA with six other future astronauts for the Mercury flights.

The cabin was a cone nearly 9 feet high, with a base diameter of 6 feet. Glenn had just enough space to sit inside in a seat molded in the shape of his body. Three retrorockets were attached to the rear of the cabin, and the parachutes to the front. Wearing a spacesuit, Glenn breathed pure oxygen.

An American in Space

A few months after the flight of Vostok 1, the Americans successfully launched the enormous rocket, Atlas, from the space vessel, Mercury. On February 20, 1962, John Glenn, seated inside Mercury's cabin, circled Earth three times in 4 hours and 55 minutes. Then three retrorockets slowed the cabin's speed while it re-entered Earth's atmosphere and separated from its protective heat shield. At 19,685 feet above the earth, its first parachute opened, then the second at 9,843 feet. Finally, the cabin landed in the ocean where Glenn was retrieved by an American naval ship.

CONQUERING THE MOON

From 1961 to 1969, the Americans worked toward and accomplished the fabulous goal of traveling 236,128 miles to the moon. This project required a highly detailed preparation of both people and equipment. Probes were sent to the moon to determine if a vessel could land there. To train men, the Gemini space capsules were launched into space carrying astronauts. After twelve trials from 1964 to 1966, we learned how to send men into space.

Saturn 5

It takes a very powerful rocket to launch a manned vessel to the moon. The Americans built the gigantic Saturn 5: three stages totaling 364 feet and weighing 2,770 tons. At its summit, it carried the space vessel, Apollo 11, weighing 45 tons and consisting of three compartments called modules. Three astronauts traveled in the command module, Columbia. Then, to land on the moon, two of them moved into the lunar module, called the LM, while the third astronaut stayed inside Columbia, circling the moon.

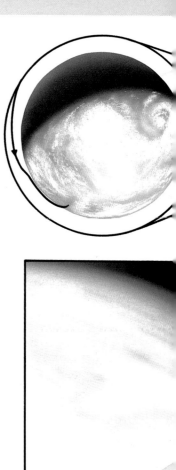

Above, the third stage of the rocket releases the LM and the Columbia module.

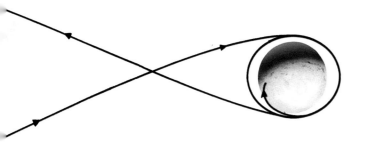

Round Trip Around the Moon

At Christmas, 1968, for the first time in history, a manned space vessel circled the moon, 69.6 miles above its surface. Launched by the powerful rocket, Saturn 5, on December 21, Apollo 8 traveled to the moon in two and a-half days, circled behind it and returned on December 27, landing in the Pacific.

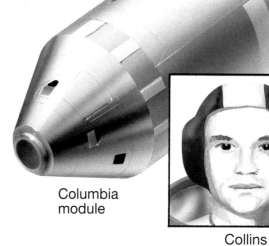

Columbia module

Collins

LM

Two Men on the Moon

On July 16, 1969, at 2:32 P.M., the Americans, Aldrin, Armstrong, and Collins, lifted off in Apollo 11, launched by Saturn 5. During the voyage, the vessel's front containing the three men, turned over and attached to the LM's side. The third stage was abandoned. As the vessel neared the moon, Aldrin and Armstrong moved into the LM (Collins stayed inside Columbia), which landed on July 20 at 9:17 P.M. on the moon's Sea of Tranquility. On July 21 at 3:56 A.M., Armstrong stepped onto the moon, realizing one of man's greatest dreams!

Armstrong

Aldrin

MEN ON THE MOON

After the triumph of Apollo 11, astronauts continued to explore the moon's surface to make new discoveries. Between 1969 and 1972, there were six other Apollo missions, only one of which, Apollo 13, failed. The astronauts explored craters and brought back rock samples for study. The last moon landing was in December, 1972. Two astronauts, one a geologist, traveled 22 miles on the moon in a jeep, collecting 249 pounds of rocks. Since 1969, twelve men have gone to the moon!

Roving the Moon

Beginning with the Apollo 15 mission, instead of traveling on foot astronauts used a jeep, the Lunar Rover, to carry equipment and rock samples. The jeep cruised at 10 miles per hour over a distance of 57 miles. It was equipped with a television camera and a dish antenna that transmitted images. Eventually astronauts increased their time on the moon from two hours and a-half in 1969, to 22 hours in 1972.

To commemorate the success of the Apollo 11 mission, astronauts planted the American flag on the moon on July 21, 1969.

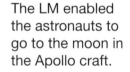

The LM enabled the astronauts to go to the moon in the Apollo craft.

The Lunar Rover ran on two large batteries. Each wheel was independent and was turned by an electric motor.

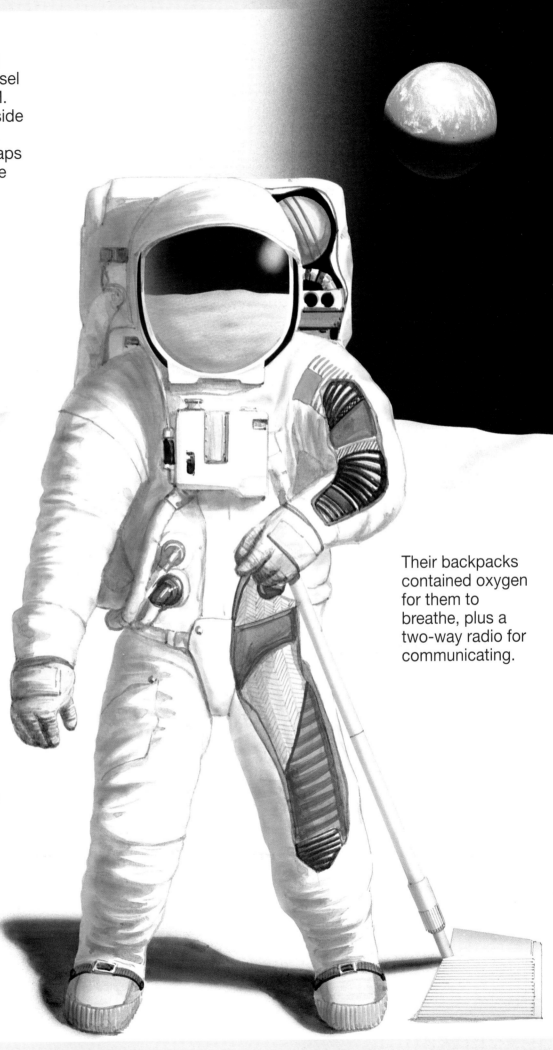

The astronauts traveled between the Apollo vessel and the moon in the LM. There were no seats inside the LM. The astronauts were suspended by straps so that the LM would be lighter.

Before stepping outside, the astronauts dressed in a 42-pound, three-layered spacesuit that helped their bodies maintain the right temperature and protected them from radiation.

Their backpacks contained oxygen for them to breathe, plus a two-way radio for communicating.

The astronauts left behind instruments which continue to take measurements for learning more about the moon. An antenna transmits the information to Earth.

SPACE SHUTTLES

Around 1970, the Americans constructed space shuttles: enormous airplanes (orbiters) that could be reused, unlike rockets which were destroyed at the end of a mission. Shuttles could carry huge satellites in a vast cargo bay (storage space), as well as return to Earth carrying teams of 6 to 7 men. Shuttles were attached to a mammoth fuel tank that fed the engines and two rocket boosters. Launched on April 12, 1981, the first shuttle, Columbia, made a two-day voyage in outer space. After this success, shuttles completed 24 missions from 1981 to 1985.

On January 28, 1986, the shuttle, Challenger, exploded at liftoff. In 1988, the Russians launched their shuttle, Burane.

The Flight of the Columbia Shuttle

Let's imagine Columbia as it readies for liftoff. This shuttle is an enormous space orbiter120 feet long, weighing 70 tons. It is attached to a huge tank filled with 700 tons of liquid fuel, with two powder-filled rocket boosters on each side. Columbia's cargo bay is 60 feet long and holds a satellite.

The two rockets and principal engines are ignited, the 200-ton shuttle lifts off. Two minutes later, 30 miles above our planet, both boosters detach, falling to Earth to be retrieved. The principal engine of the shuttle, fed by the fuel tank, functions at full speed to carry the shuttle beyond the atmosphere. Nine minutes after liftoff, the empty external fuel tank is released. It will break apart in space. The shuttle's principal engines are then ignited by internal fuel tanks.

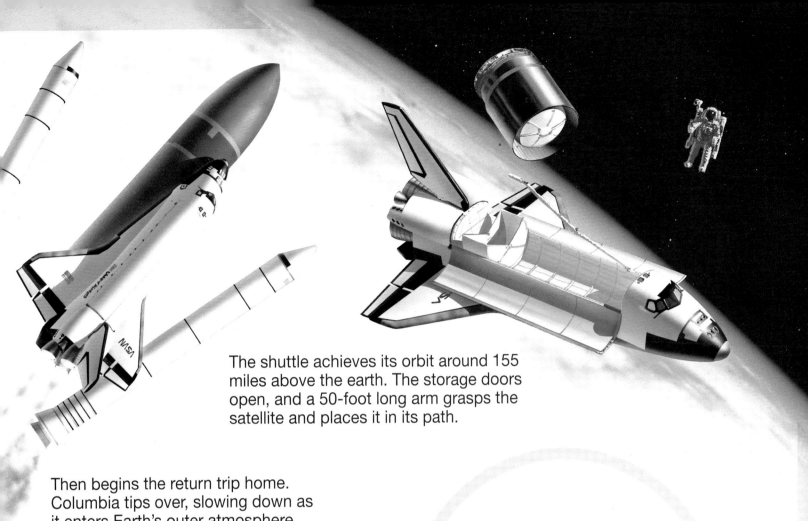

The shuttle achieves its orbit around 155 miles above the earth. The storage doors open, and a 50-foot long arm grasps the satellite and places it in its path.

Then begins the return trip home. Columbia tips over, slowing down as it enters Earth's outer atmosphere. At 75 miles altitude, flying at 17,000 miles per hour, its contact with the air creates an intense heat, but the shuttle is well-protected by a layer of heatproof tiles. The shuttle continues to brake, slowing down until its rocket engines stop.

At about 28 miles above ground, Columbia, flown like an airplane but by astronauts, begins the long glide toward a touchdown runway where it must land at a speed of 240 miles per hour. The shuttle first descends at a steep angle, then straightens up at 1640 feet above ground. Its landing gear lowers, then it rolls along the runway for about a mile and a-half before stopping. A few minutes later, the team step out, home again on Earth.

LAUNCHERS

Launchers are rockets that send satellites into space. So that these rockets can break away from Earth's pull, they must be very powerful and fly at 17,000 miles per hour. They are enormous metal cylinders, 100 to 200 feet tall, made of three levels (stages). A satellite sits at the top of the rocket. Each stage has one or several engines, with fuel tanks. As it burns, the fuel emits a gas which makes the rocket lift off, then propes It into space. Once the fuel is burned, the stages detach one after another.

Ariane 1 could launch satellites weighing 4,000 pounds to 22,000 feet. In 1999, Ariane 5 will launch a load weighing more than 15,000 pounds.

The Ariane Rocket

The European rocket, Ariane, has already launched 140 satellites since its first launch in 1979. The rockets have become more powerful and send heavier and heavier satellites.

The Launch

Every launch of Ariane takes place in Kourou in French Guiana. In the control room, technicians follow on their television and computer monitors the progress of the launch. Before the liftoff, everything is carefully checked: engines, security systems, and radio connections. Then, the engines are ignited: four booster propellers at the bottom of the rocket. The rocket lifts off vertically and rises for 12 seconds until it's 23 miles above ground. At that point, the boosters are released.

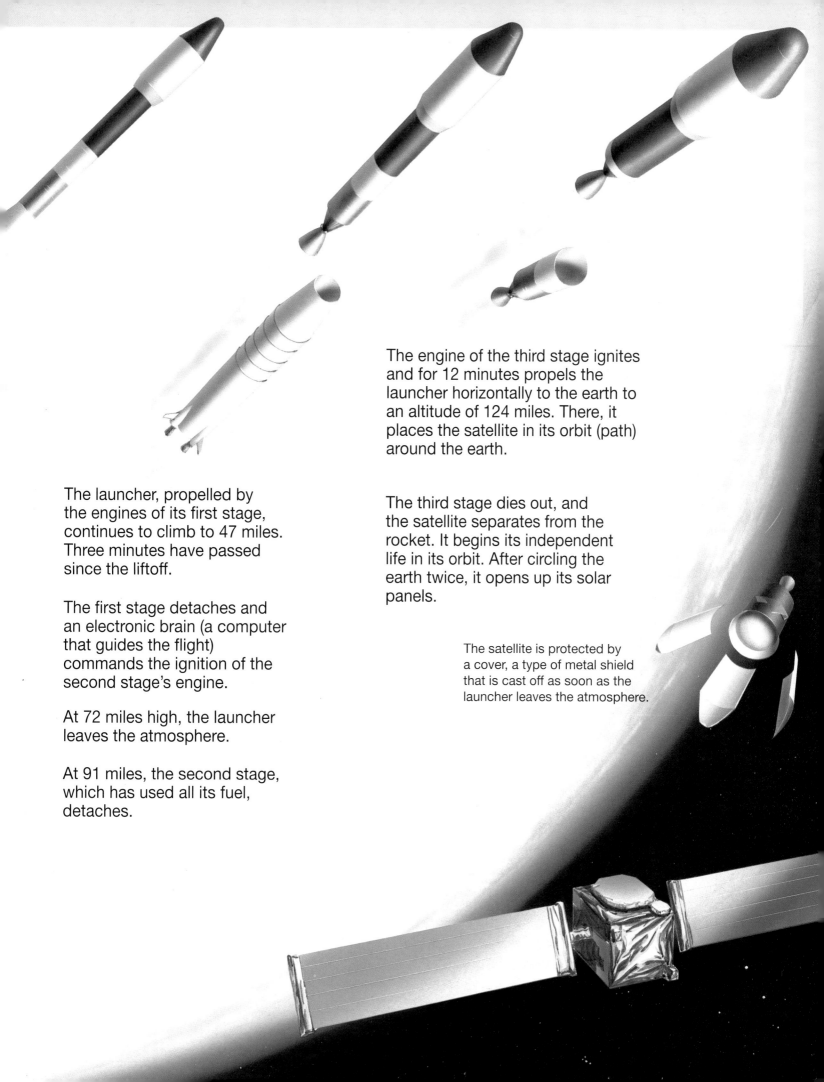

The engine of the third stage ignites and for 12 minutes propels the launcher horizontally to the earth to an altitude of 124 miles. There, it places the satellite in its orbit (path) around the earth.

The launcher, propelled by the engines of its first stage, continues to climb to 47 miles. Three minutes have passed since the liftoff.

The first stage detaches and an electronic brain (a computer that guides the flight) commands the ignition of the second stage's engine.

At 72 miles high, the launcher leaves the atmosphere.

At 91 miles, the second stage, which has used all its fuel, detaches.

The third stage dies out, and the satellite separates from the rocket. It begins its independent life in its orbit. After circling the earth twice, it opens up its solar panels.

The satellite is protected by a cover, a type of metal shield that is cast off as soon as the launcher leaves the atmosphere.

MAN IN SPACE

Astronauts who travel in shuttles or work in space stations must adjust to an environment where everything is different: objects, no longer pulled by the earth, have no weight. They don't fall, they float. Astronauts must learn how to live in a weightless state. In space their bodies float, their muscles weaken, and their heads swell, but once adapted, they can stay for months. The cosmonaut, A. Leonov, was the first to step into outer space. What an experience!

Thanks to a motorized seat, an astronaut can move up to 33 feet away from the shuttle. This seat weighs 330 pounds and is equipped with 24 small, compressed-gas jet engines. By manipulating hand controls, he can move in any direction.

Stepping into Space

Let's take a walk in space with an astronaut as he leaves his vessel to repair a satellite. Before going out, he puts on a spacesuit made of several layers of insulation that protect him from the cold, sunlight, and small flying rocks. In the material, tubes filled with water maintain the right body temperature. His backpack supplies enough oxygen for him to breathe for six hours in space.

Sleeping in the Shuttle

To sleep, an astronaut slides into a sleeping bag attached to the side of the cabin so that he doesn't float. It doesn't matter if he sleeps vertically or horizontally: There is no longer any sense of direction. His muscles do not rest as well as they do in a bed however, so he often wakes up with backaches!

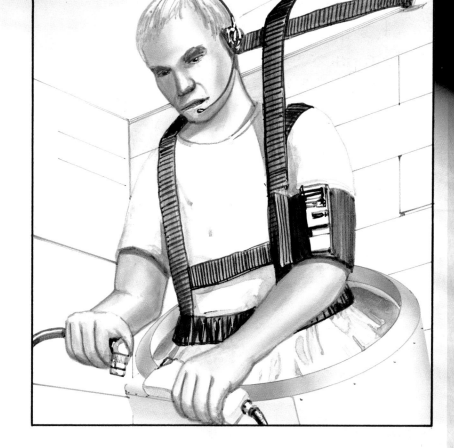

A Laboratory 220 Miles above Earth

Inside orbital stations, experiments in weightlessness are possible in laboratories. New medicines and crystals are produced there. Astronauts connect instruments to their bodies to see how they react in space. They measure their blood pressure and heartbeat. They record astronomical observations and do experiments with animals and plants. Throughout, they must attach their instruments with elastic belts so that they don't float around the cabin.

Meals in Space

Eating in a weightless environment is difficult, because food floats inside the cabin! This is why it is put inside small plastic bags, tin cans, or reduced to a powder. Drinking in space is also a problem. Juice being poured into a glass will break up into small bubbles, so astronauts suck their drinks through a small tube.

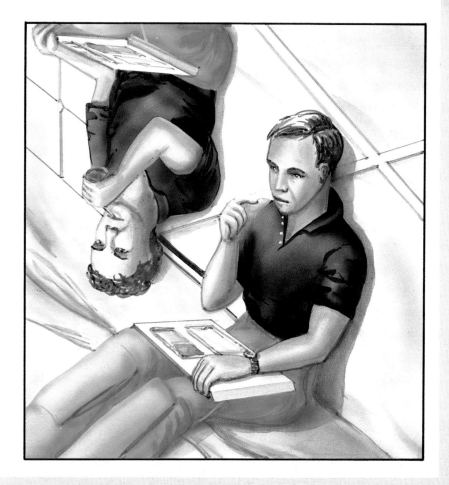

SPACE STATIONS

Space stations are laboratories where astronauts live while circling 185 or 250 miles above the earth. Since 1957, nine stations have been launched into space, but only the Russian station Mir is still in service. Put into orbit on February 19, 1986, Mir is 50 feet long and weighs 20 tons. Teams of two to six cosmonauts spend a week to several months in Mir to do scientific experiments.

The Mir Station

Mir is composed of several compartments called modules. A large room is located in the center which serves as the piloting, work, rest, and sports entertainment station. For sleeping, the cosmonauts have individual cabins. Other modules, serving as scientific laboratories, are attached around the central cabin. Mir can be enlarged.

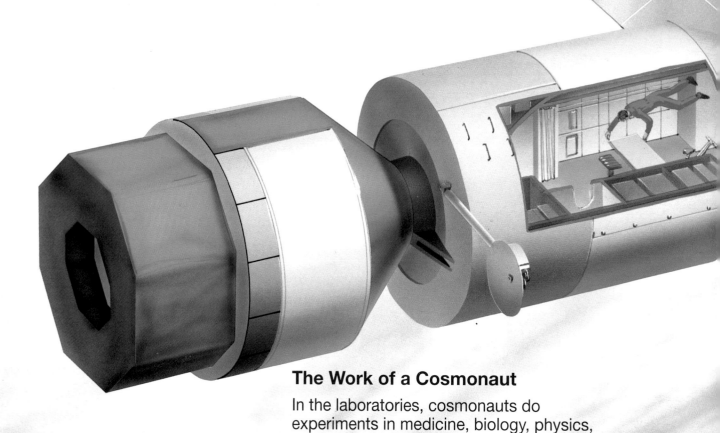

The Work of a Cosmonaut

In the laboratories, cosmonauts do experiments in medicine, biology, physics, and astronomy. Their activities are followed on Earth by radio and video. At the end of a mission, they bring back photographs and films.

The Vessel Progress

Every four to six weeks, the vessel, Progress, travels to Mir to replenish fresh produce and water for cosmonauts staying for a long time in Mir. It also brings needed materials for their experiments.

As an experiment, the Russians equipped some Progress vessels with a 65-foot wide mirror for capturing sunlight. Why? To be able in the future to send sunlight to cities which exist in polar darkness. Time will tell if this is possible to accomplish.

The Vessel

A Round Trip for Mir

Cosmonauts fly to Mir in the vessel Soyuz, launched from Baïkonur in central Asia. The flight takes two days. For the return trip, the team uses the prior team's vessel that is tied to the station.

The Vessel Soyuz

SATELLITES

Satellites are man-made objects launched into space by rockets. Most circle the earth, others orbit around the sun and the planets. These mini-laboratories are equipped with machines which receive and send information by radio signals to stations on Earth. Some make scientific observations, others help us communicate from one country to another. Depending on their mission, satellites circle at different altitudes: the closest at 125 miles and the furthest at 2,200 miles.

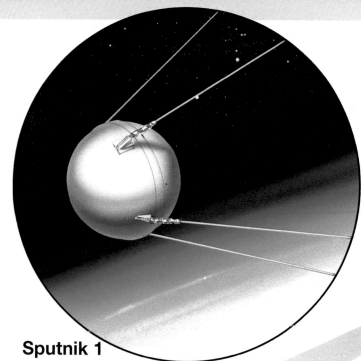

Sputnik 1

The first satellite ever launched was Sputnik 1 by Russia on October 4, 1957. This small sphere, 23 inches wide and equipped with two radio transmitters, circled the earth while sending beeping signals with its long antennae.

Communication satellites enable us to telephone, send faxes, and to send television programs from one side of the earth to the other. Thus, the Olympic Games can be seen live by one to two billion television viewers.

Thanks to satellites that observe the earth, we can draw accurate maps of all the continents, oceans, forests, and mountains. They can also fly over hard-to-reach regions, such as our deserts, and help discover oil deposits.

Navigation satellites fly over the oceans. They chart the movement of icebergs, locate sailboats in races and ships in trouble. Between 1985 and 1990, more than a thousand people were saved by satellites.

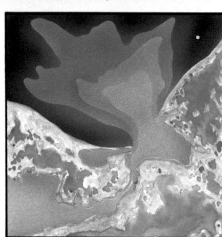

Satellites have different shapes, sizes and weights depending on their missions. They are equipped with telescopes, two-way radios, cameras, and measuring devices.

Just as a mirror reflects light rays, the reflectors of a satellite send radio waves from a sending station to a receiving station. We call these relay satellites. They send messages from one station to another over the ocean.

The satellite antenna is used to exchange information with the earth. Its solar panels provide energy for making it work.

Military satellites help us safely observe military installations and operations (airplane, ship and troop movements, and nuclear testing) of another country. From 93 miles above the earth, a camera with a telephoto lens can see 3-inch details!

Weather satellites photograph cloud activity that surrounds the earth and send these images to weather stations. Thanks to them, specialists can create weather maps and predict the weather.

Astronomical satellites are observatories launched deep into outer space. With their space telescopes, they can send us images of the planets and the sun. Before we had such satellites, we only knew what space we could see from the earth.

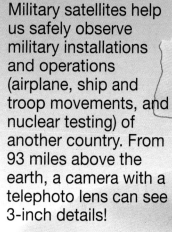

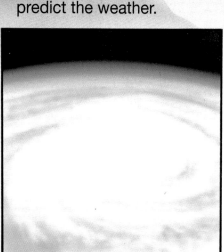

SPACE PROBES

Space probes are are unmanned vehicles that we send into space to explore the planets of our solar system by flying over them or landing in places where we cannot yet go. They take photographs, measurements, and soil samples that they send back in small rockets. Since the distances are very long, we wait months, even years, to receive their images. Space probes first explored the closest planets (Venus, Mercury, and Mars), then the furthest away, such as Jupiter.

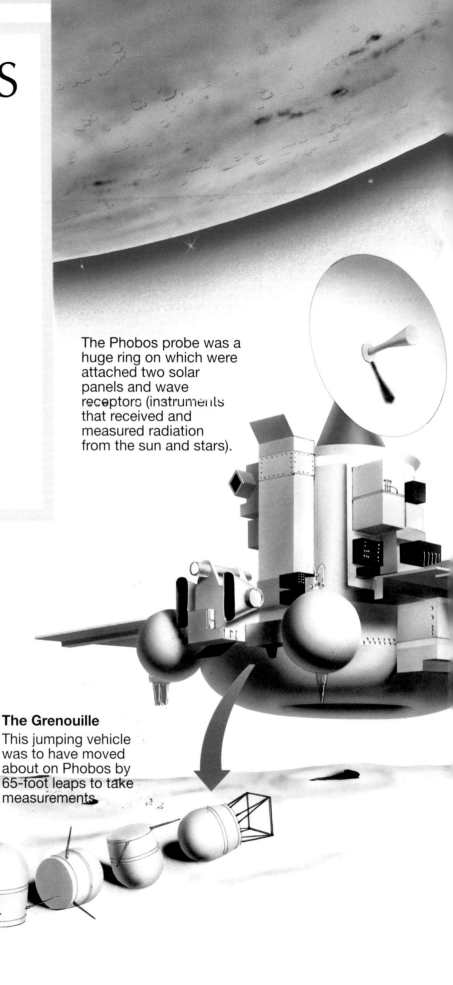

The Phobos probe was a huge ring on which were attached two solar panels and wave receptors (instruments that received and measured radiation from the sun and stars).

The Phobos Project

Just as the moon circles around the earth, Phobos is a huge rock that circles around the planet Mars. It is a natural satellite. To learn more about the soil and environment of Mars, the Phobos project sent two probes in 1988 to orbit around Mars by following Phobos. Two space vehicles, the Atterrisseur ("the touchdown") and the Grenouille ("the frog") were meant to come out of the probe and land on Phobos soil.

The Grenouille

This jumping vehicle was to have moved about on Phobos by 65-foot leaps to take measurements.

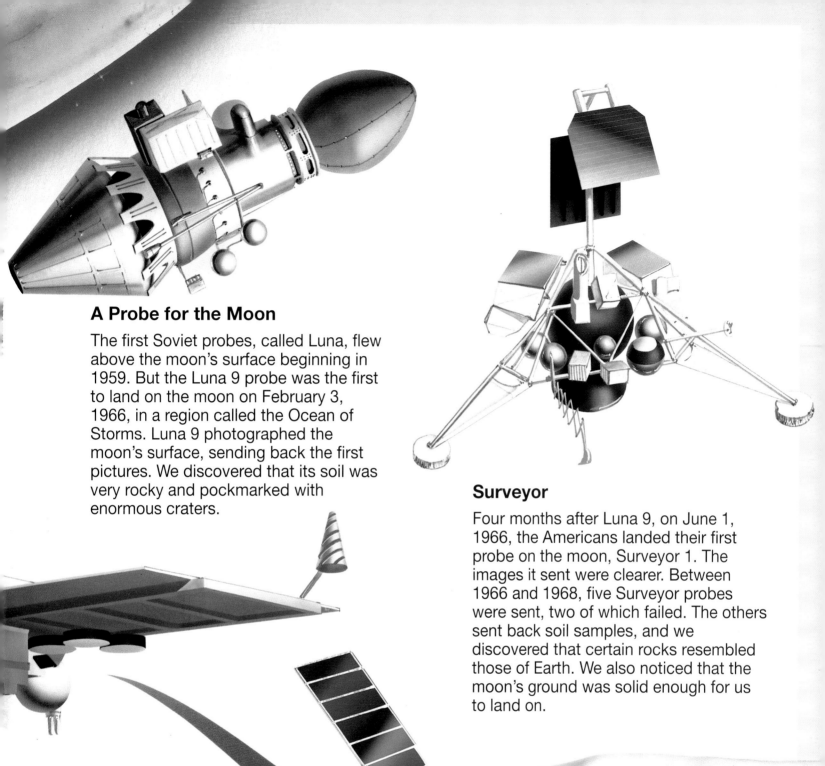

A Probe for the Moon

The first Soviet probes, called Luna, flew above the moon's surface beginning in 1959. But the Luna 9 probe was the first to land on the moon on February 3, 1966, in a region called the Ocean of Storms. Luna 9 photographed the moon's surface, sending back the first pictures. We discovered that its soil was very rocky and pockmarked with enormous craters.

Surveyor

Four months after Luna 9, on June 1, 1966, the Americans landed their first probe on the moon, Surveyor 1. The images it sent were clearer. Between 1966 and 1968, five Surveyor probes were sent, two of which failed. The others sent back soil samples, and we discovered that certain rocks resembled those of Earth. We also noticed that the moon's ground was solid enough for us to land on.

The Results of the Phobos Project

The first probe was lost. The second sent fascinating information and images of the sun and especially of the soil and surface of Mars. Then it was lost before it could set its vehicles on Phobos as planned.

The Atterrisseur

This other vehicle was designed to attach itself to the ground of Phobos by an anchor, and to unfold three arms formed by solar panels supplying its energy. Its function was to explore the soil of Phobos.

THE FUTURE

One day, we hope to place astronauts permanently in space stations. One huge international station, called Freedom, will contain two American modules, a Japanese module, and a European module, Columbus. The Ariane 5 rocket will place Columbus in orbit at 288 miles above the earth, and the astronauts will arrive at Freedom in a space plane called Hermès. Unlike a shuttle, this plane will not be able to launch satellites, but will only transport three men and their material. In the station, small factories will work in a weightless environment to reveal the mysteries of outer space.

A Station on the Moon

Astronauts have not returned to the moon since 1972. As we enter the twenty-first century, new missions are being planned with the construction of a permanent lunar base. The moon will become a scientific observatory. Laboratories will study the moon and its history, and telescopes will peer at its hidden side.

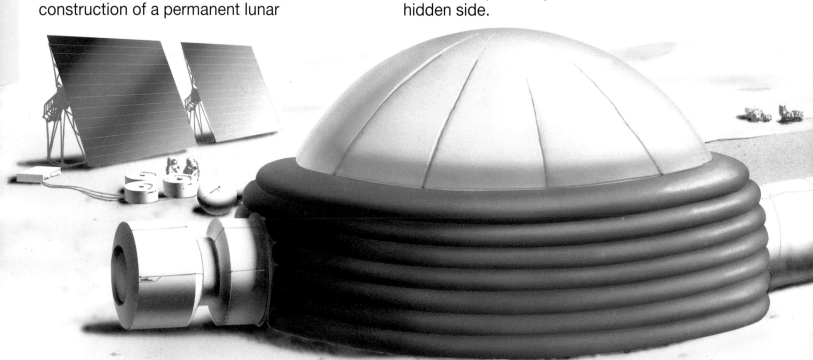

Probes for Saturn
(left)

The Americans sent the first probes to Saturn from 1980 to 1981: Voyager 1 and 2 sent back 18,000 images of the planet and gave information on its rings and the diameter of its satellite Titan. To learn more about Saturn and Titan's atmosphere, the Cassini/Huygens probes were sent in 1997. This was a shared project between the United States and Europe.

Mars, Here We Come!
(pictured at right)

After the moon, the conquest of Mars is our greatest goal. Around 2030, man hopes to land on Mars in a huge vessel and explore the planet. The voyage to Mars would take more than 300 days, but this project is extremely expensive and poses many medical and technical problems. Until then, we will send scientific observation stations to Mars and automatic vehicles which will take photographs and send us information. Later, small rockets will send back samples of the soil.

ISBN 2-215-06174-X
© Éditions FLEURUS, Paris, 1998.
Printed in Italy.